THE DAMN FINE COLORING BOOK

UNOFFICIAL TWIN PEAKS INSPIRED COLOR THERAPY

ADULT COLOR THERAPY

M. CRYPTKEEPER

ISBN: 1548140007

ISBN-13: 978-1548140007

INTRODUCTION

COLOR IN VARIOUS ICONIC QUOTES AND IMAGERY INSPIRED BY TWIN PEAKS.

EACH PAGE IS DOUBLED SO YOU'LL BE ABLE TO KEEP AN ORIGINAL OUTLINE TO SCAN OR COPY FOR FUTURE COLORING USE.

GRAB A SLICE OF CHERRY PIE AND CUP OF DAMN FINE COFFEE AND START COLORING.

HAND DRAWN ILLUSTRATIONS BY M. CRYPTKEEPER.

CONTENTS

TWIN PEAKS

WHAT IS TWIN PEAKS? IT'S AN AMERICAN SERIAL DRAMA TELEVISION SERIES. CREATED BY DAVID LYNCH AND MARK FROST THAT FIRST PREMIERED ON APRIL THE 8TH, 1990. IT WAS ONE OF THE MOST TOP-RATED SERIES OF 1990, HOWEVER DECLINING RATINGS LED TO IT BEING CANCELLED AFTER ITS SECOND SEASON (IN 1991). IT GAINED A CULT FOLLOWING. TWIN PEAKS HAS OFTEN BEEN LISTED AMONG THE GREATEST TELEVISION DRAMAS OF ALL TIME.

THE SERIES FOLLOWS AN INVESTIGATION LEAD BY FBI SPECIAL AGENT DALE COOPER (PLAYED BY KYLE MACLACHLAN) INTO THE MURDER OF HOMECOMING QUEEN LAURA PALMER (PLAYED BY SHERYL LEE) IN THE FICTIONAL TOWN CALLED TWIN PEAKS (WASHINGTON).

IN THIS BOOK YOU'LL BE ABLE TO COLOR IN VARIOUS ICONIC QUOTES AND IMAGERY INSPIRED BY TWIN PEAKS. GRAB A SLICE OF CHERRY PIE AND CUP OF DAMN FINE COFFEE AND START COLORING.

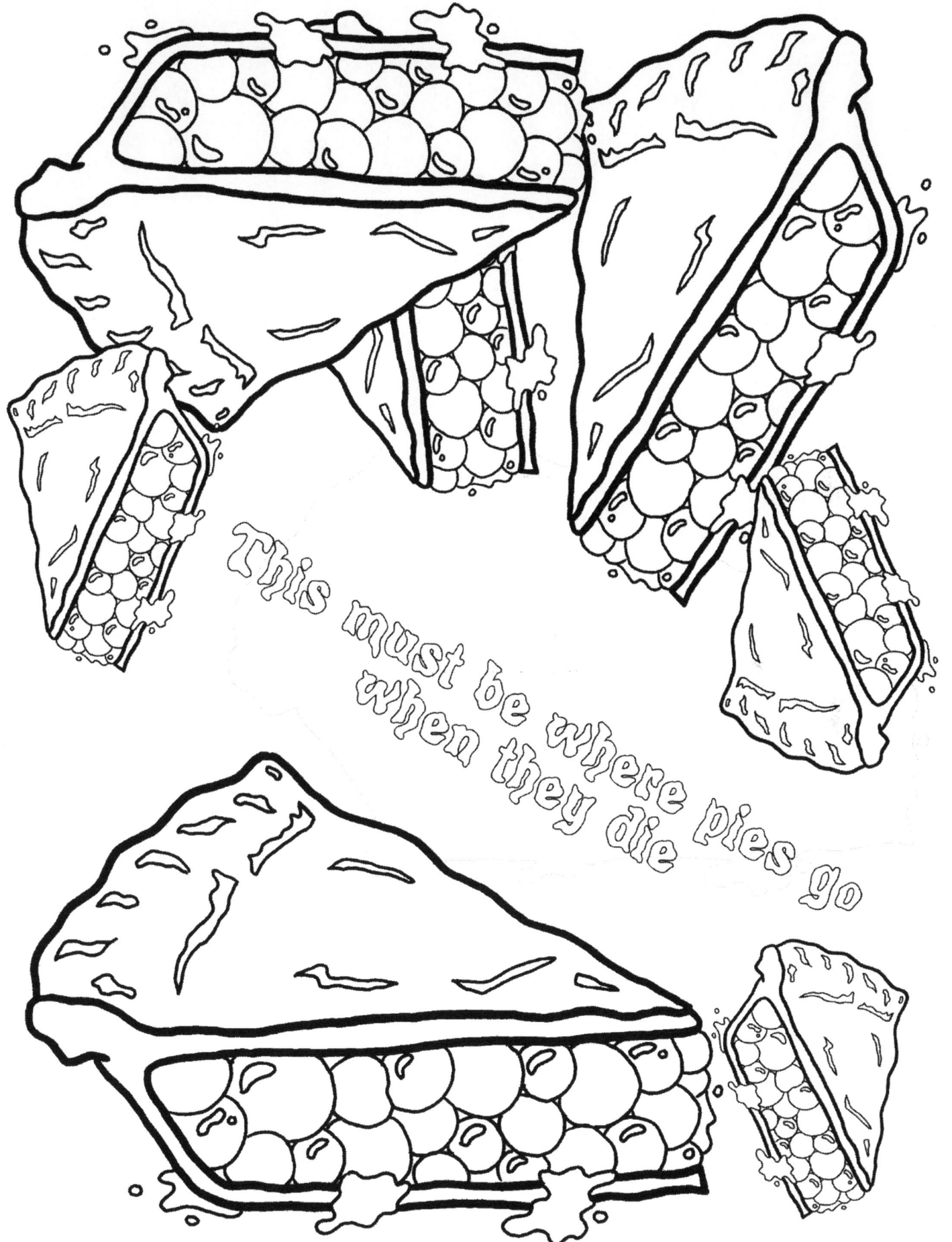

This must be where pies go when they die

This page has been kept blank to prevent pen **BLEEDING.**

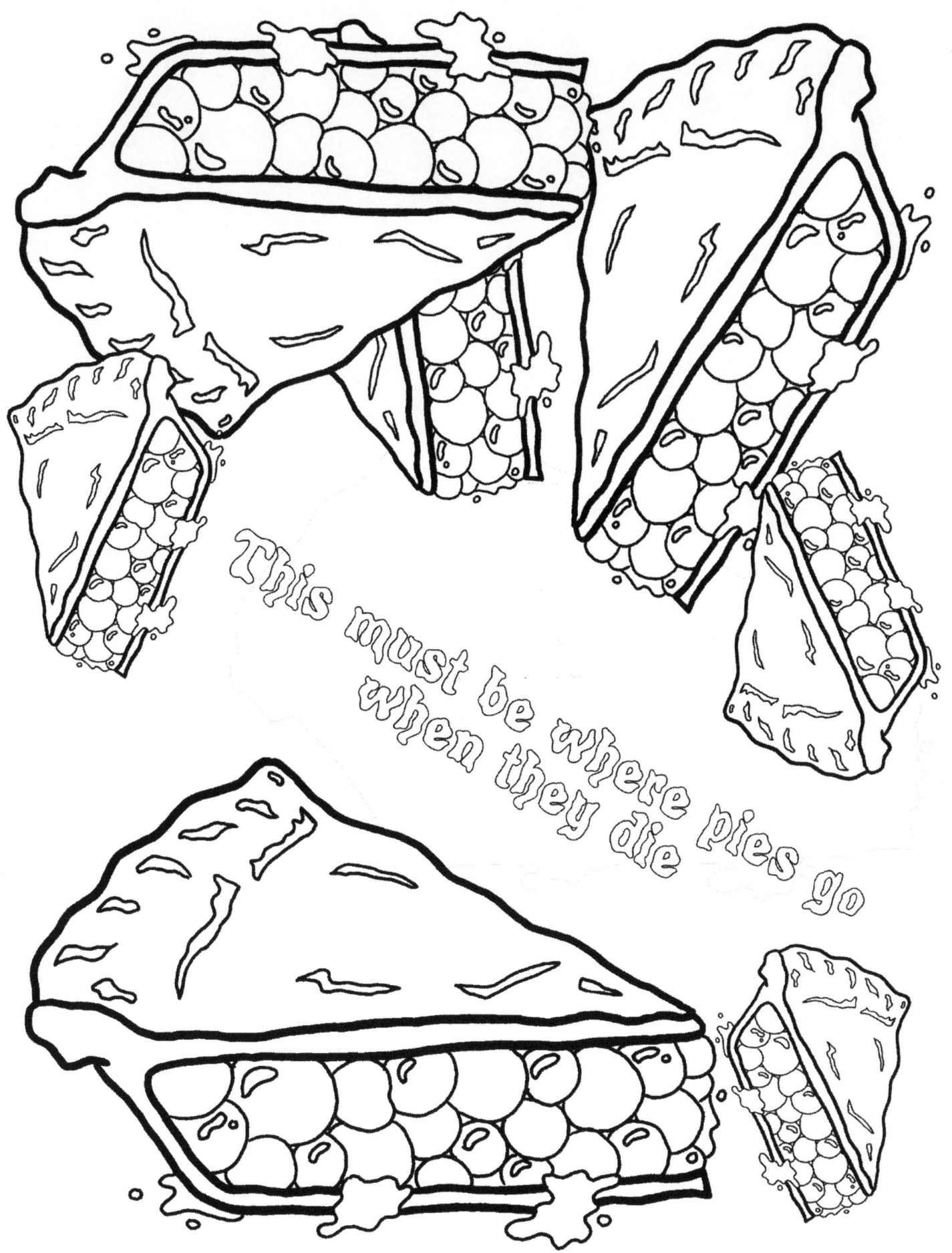

This must be where pies go when they die

This page has been kept blank to prevent pen BLEEDING.

This page has been kept blank to prevent pen BLEEDING.

This page has been kept blank to prevent pen BLEEDING.

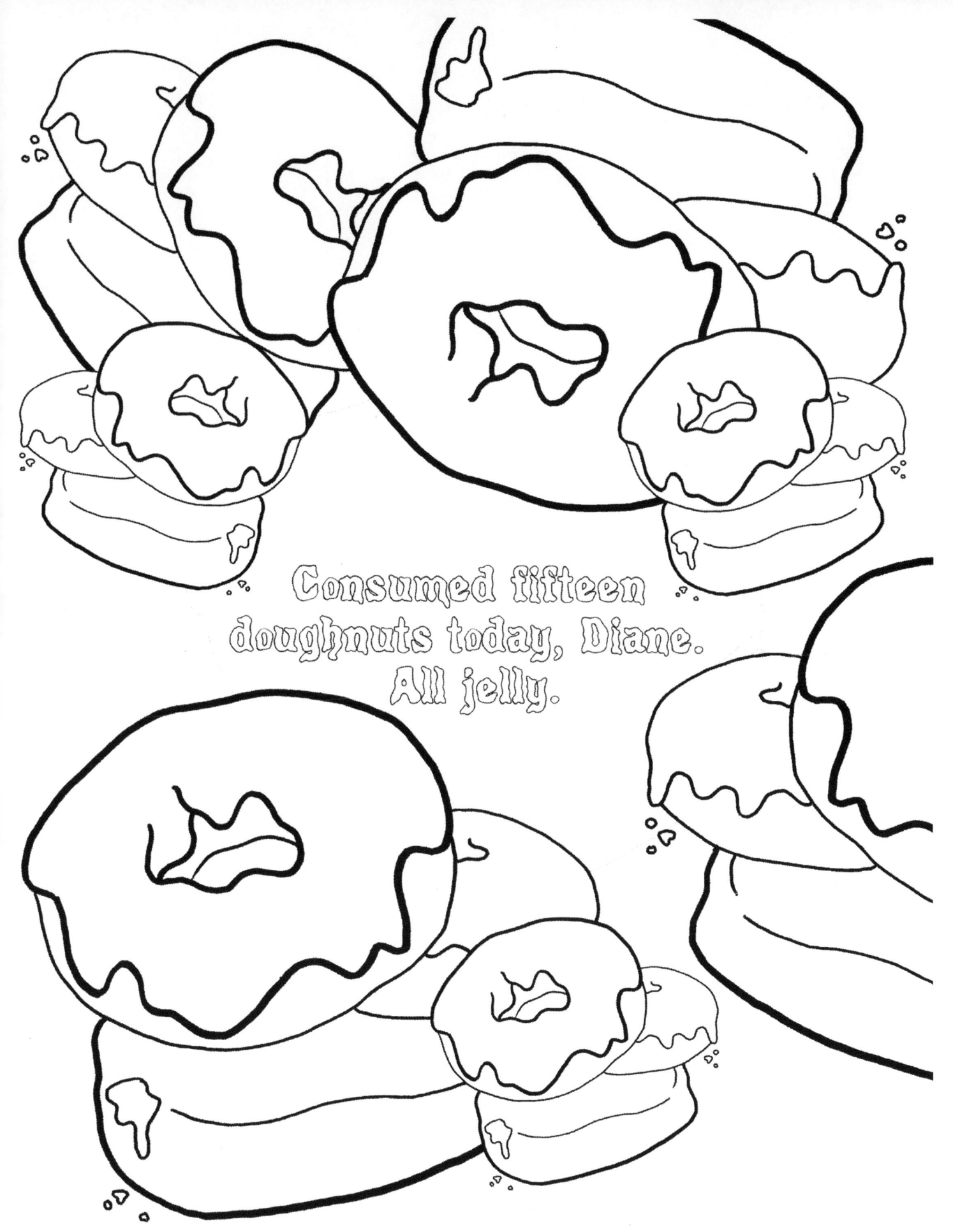

Consumed fifteen doughnuts today, Diane. All jelly.

This page has been kept blank to prevent pen **BLEEDING.**

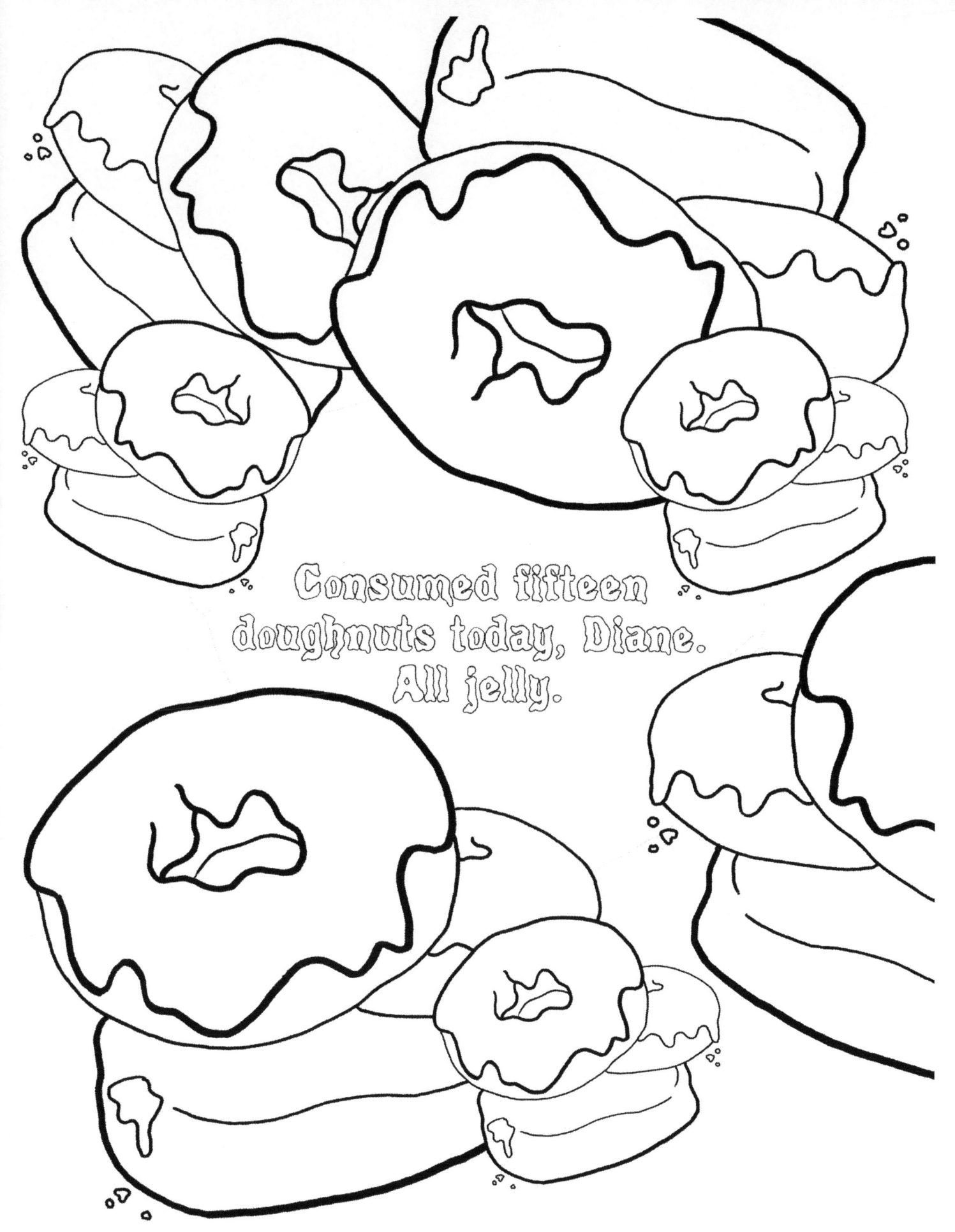

Consumed fifteen doughnuts today, Diane. All jelly.

This page has been kept blank to prevent pen BLEEDING.

Through the darkness of future past
The magician longs to see.
One chants out between two worlds
Fire walk with me.

This page has been kept blank to prevent pen BLEEDING.

Through the darkness of future past
The magician longs to see.
One chants out between two worlds
Fire walk with me.

This page has been kept blank to prevent pen BLEEDING.

This page has been kept blank to prevent pen BLEEDING.

This page has been kept blank to prevent pen **BLEEDING.**

This page has been kept blank to prevent pen BLEEDING.

This page has been kept blank to prevent pen BLEEDING.

This page has been kept blank to prevent pen BLEEDING.

I only have time for coffee.

You know, this is – excuse me – a damn fine cup of coffee.

This page has been kept blank to prevent pen BLEEDING.

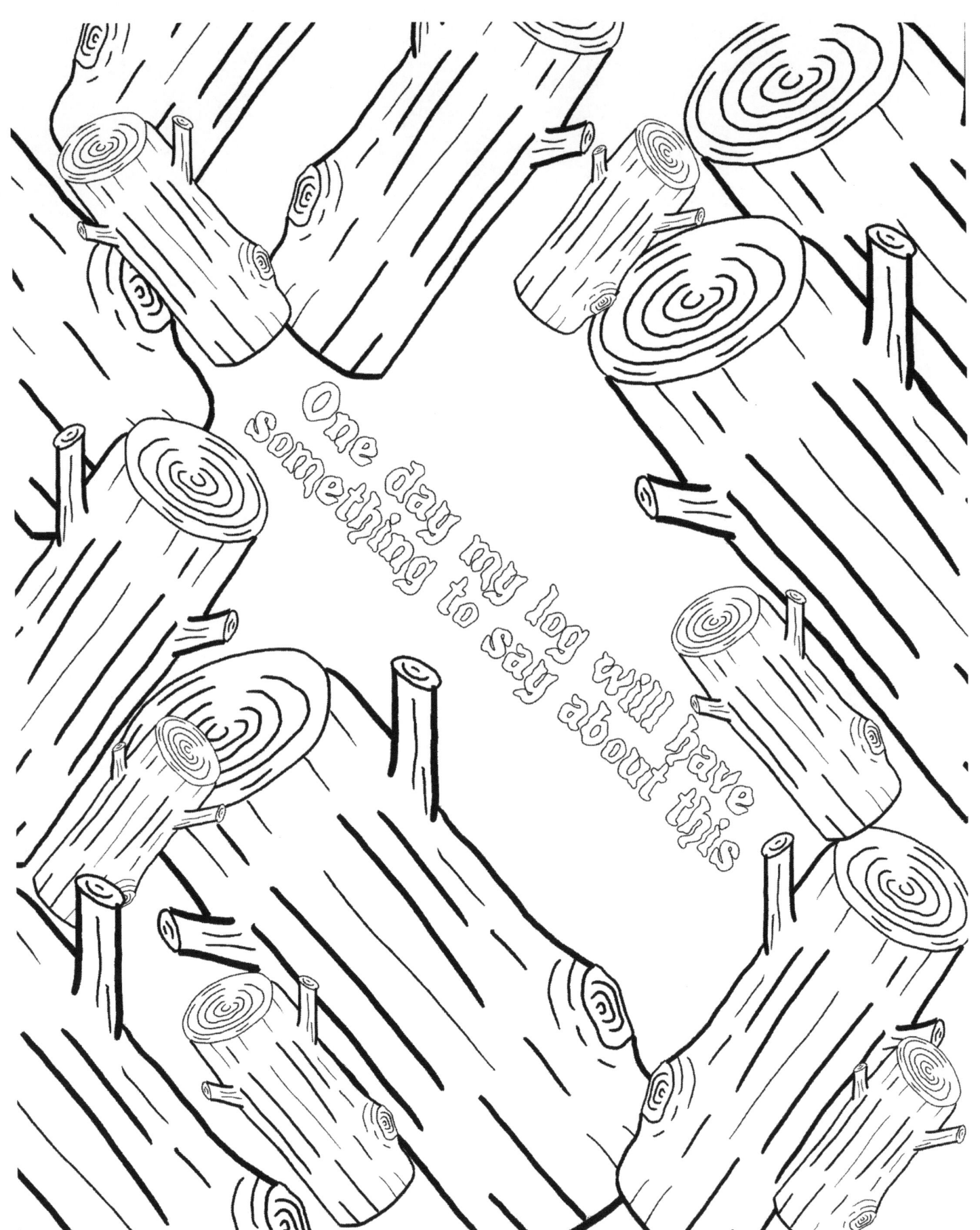

This page has been kept blank to prevent pen BLEEDING.

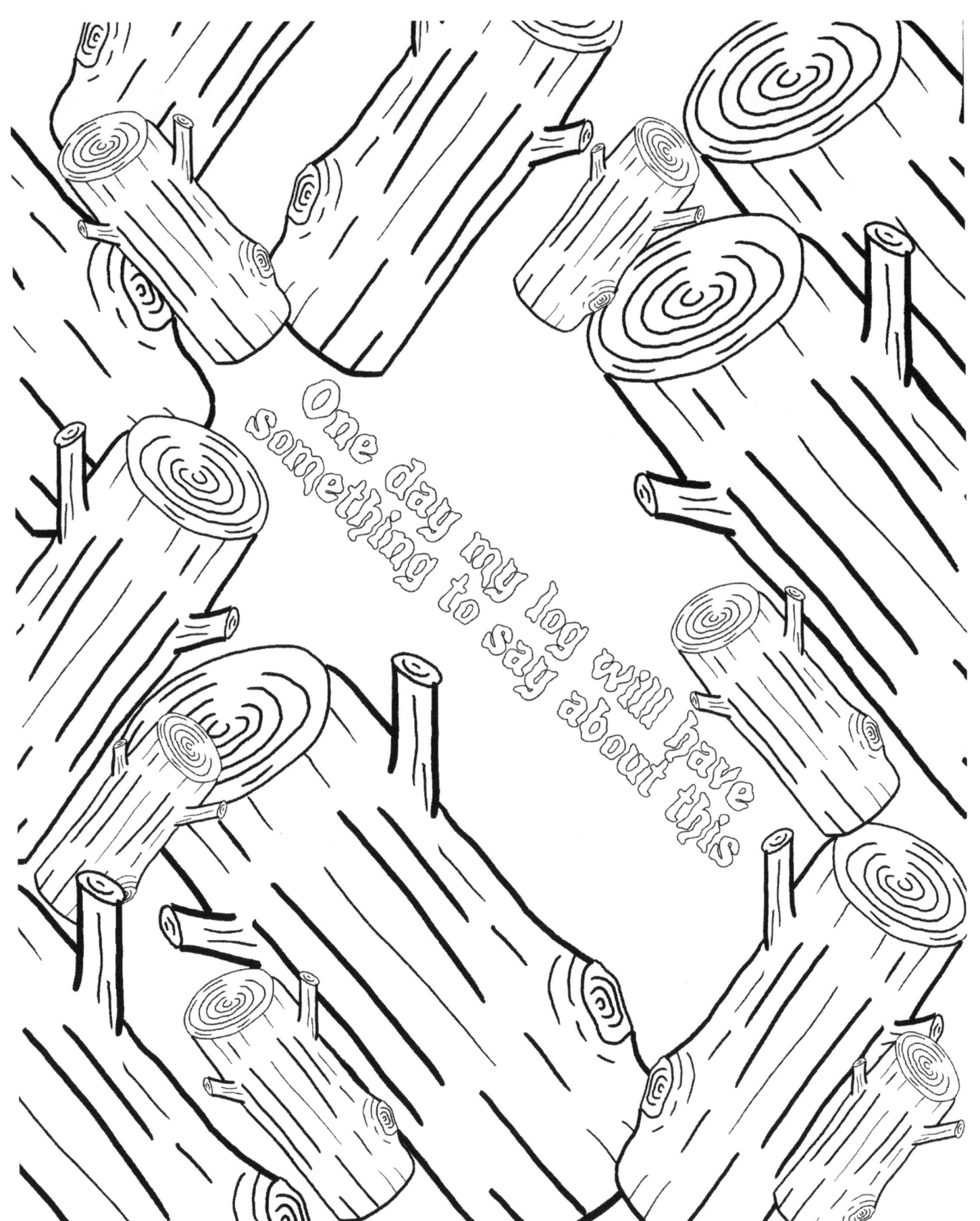

This page has been kept blank to prevent pen BLEEDING.

This page has been kept blank to prevent pen BLEEDING.

This page has been kept blank to prevent pen BLEEDING.

This page has been kept blank to prevent pen BLEEDING.

45

This page has been kept blank to prevent pen **BLEEDING.**

THANK YOU FOR SUPPORTING PUMPKIN PUBLICATIONS, I HOPE YOU'RE NOT TOO SPOOKED.

PLEASE LEAVE A REVIEW IF POSSIBLE, AS YOUR FEEDBACK IS MUCH APPRECIATED.

ABOUT THE AUTHOR

M. CRYPTKEEPER IS A GRADUATED ART STUDENT BASED IN THE UNITED KINGDOM (LONDON ESSEX). WITH A PASSION FOR ILLUSTRATION AND HORROR IT ONLY MADE SENSE FOR HER TO START PUMPKIN PUBLICATIONS: AN INDIE BOOK COMPANY THAT SPECIALIZES IN MODERN HORROR FOLK TALES AND HAND DRAWN COLOUR THERAPY. HER QUIRKY STYLE INSTANTLY TRANSLATES INTO HER BOOKS CREATING A TRULY IMMERSIVE EXPERIENCE.

Printed in Poland
by Amazon Fulfillment
Poland Sp. z o.o., Wrocław